Why Women Deserve Better

Daria Gałek

WHY WOMEN DESERVE BETTER

First edition. June 24, 2023.

Copyright © 2023 Daria Gałek.

ISBN: 979-8223030430

Written by Daria Gałek.

Table of Contents

Introduction

Welcome to the book dedicated to the important and timely topic of gender equality. In the pages that follow, we will embark on a journey through the various dimensions of gender equality, exploring its significance, challenges, and the actions required to achieve a more equitable world.

Gender equality is a fundamental human right and a cornerstone of a just and inclusive society. It encompasses equal rights, opportunities, and treatment for people of all genders, challenging the deeply rooted norms and stereotypes that have perpetuated gender-based discrimination and inequality for centuries. While progress has been made in many areas, there is still much work to be done to dismantle the barriers that hinder true equality.

This book aims to shed light on the multifaceted aspects of gender equality, examining its impact on education, the workforce, politics, law, family life, and beyond. By delving into these diverse domains, we hope to foster a comprehensive understanding of the challenges we face and the strategies required to effect meaningful change.

Throughout this book, we will explore the importance of empowering women and girls, dismantling systemic biases, promoting inclusive policies, and fostering a culture of respect and equal opportunities for all. We will delve into the ways in which gender equality intersects with other dimensions of identity, such as race, ethnicity, class, and sexuality, recognizing the interconnections that shape our experiences.

Moreover, this book seeks to inspire and ignite action. It aims to empower individuals, communities, and institutions to become catalysts for change, recognizing that achieving gender equality is a collective effort. By highlighting inspiring stories, successful initiatives, and best practices, we hope to provide a roadmap for progress and encourage readers to take part in the transformative journey toward a more just and equitable world.

We invite you to delve into the chapters ahead, to challenge your assumptions, and to reflect on how you can contribute to the advancement of gender equality. Together, let us embark on this crucial exploration and work towards a future where gender equality is not just an aspiration, but a lived reality for all.

Chapter 1: Reclaiming the Voice

The history of humanity is filled with numerous examples of silencing women and restricting their participation in society. For centuries, a patriarchal system prevailed, marginalizing women, subjecting them to discrimination, and denying them a voice. The collective struggle for gender equality and women's rights has brought about progress, but there are still significant challenges that limit women's opportunities.

Reclaiming the voice is a crucial element in the fight for gender equality and the construction of a more just society. It involves enabling women to express their thoughts, opinions, and experiences, and creating spaces where their voices are heard and respected.

It is important to understand that reclaiming the voice is not merely about raising the volume of women's voices. It is about creating conditions in which women are actively listened to, respected, and treated as equals to men. The valuable perspectives and experiences of women are an irreplaceable source of knowledge and inspiration for society as a whole.

In reclaiming the voice lies the potential to address social inequalities and build a more equitable world. Each one of us has a role to play in this process by listening, supporting, and amplifying women's efforts towards equality. Only when we ensure the full participation of women can we build a society where every voice matters and every person has the opportunity to fulfill their potential.

1.1 History of Silencing Women

For centuries, women have been systematically silenced and marginalized. Their voices and experiences were disregarded, and societies imposed numerous restrictions and injustices upon them. This history of oppression has deep roots and continues to impact women's lives today.

From ancient times to the Middle Ages, women were often deprived of basic political rights, such as the right to vote or full participation in public life. Their access to education and knowledge was limited, hindering the development of their intellectual and professional potential. Women were frequently regarded as property of men and treated as objects expected to conform to traditional gender roles.

Many women were denied the opportunity to inherit property, manage their own wealth, or make decisions about their own lives. They had limited chances to develop their talents and abilities, and their career aspirations were often suppressed by dominant patriarchal social structures.

In the realm of culture and art as well, women were often sidelined. Their creativity and contributions to cultural development were marginalized, and their perspectives and histories remained invisible or were transformed into narratives based on stereotypes and biases.

However, despite this long history of suppression, women have always fought for their rights and dignity. Feminists and activists throughout the ages campaigned for gender equality, combating discrimination and injustices. Their efforts have led to significant social and political changes, such as gaining the right to vote, protection against violence towards women, and equal rights in the workplace.

The legacy of silencing women's voices still persists in today's society. Women continue to face unfair prejudices, discrimination, and violence. Women's voices are often still ignored or trivialized. However, increasing awareness and social activism are fostering change. Women around the world are uniting to build a society based on equality and justice, where their voices are heard, and their rights are respected.

Men also play a crucial role as allies and partners in the fight for gender equality. Strengthening gender equality requires collective effort and shedding societal constraints and stereotypes.

Overcoming the history of silencing women requires further action, such as education, social change, and the creation of supportive policies and structures for equality. By understanding and appreciating the long journey women have traversed, we can collectively build a more just and equitable society for future generations.

1.2 Female Leadership and Self-Sufficiency

Over the past decades, women have been achieving success and gaining influential positions in various fields of life. The rise of female leadership in politics, business, social sciences, and many other areas demonstrates that women have tremendous potential and much to offer to society.

Female leadership brings unique perspectives and approaches to decision-making. Women often prioritize collaboration, empathy, and peaceful conflict resolution. Their life experiences, including motherhood, caregiving, and combating discrimination, contribute to a more comprehensive and well-rounded approach to social and economic issues.

Integrating the female perspective into decision-making is crucial for building a more just and equal society. Women have the ability to recognize and address problems that affect their communities. Their voices and experiences are significant, both at the local and global levels.

Female leadership is not solely about holding high positions or having formal titles. It also involves fostering self-sufficiency and autonomy among women. Women who are aware of their value can make independent decisions and pursue their goals, contributing to social change and the advancement of equality.

The self-sufficiency of women is a key aspect of the gender equality struggle. Access to education, healthcare, professional opportunities, and financial resources is crucial for women to be independent and fulfilled in their lives. Strengthening the self-sufficiency of women requires creating conditions that facilitate their development and enable equal access to resources and opportunities.

As female leadership and self-sufficiency continue to grow, societal perceptions regarding the role and potential of women also evolve. This inspires the next generations of girls and young women, giving them hope for a better future and motivating them to strive for their goals.

In summary, the rise of female leadership and self-sufficiency is a crucial element in the fight for gender equality. Women bring unique perspectives and experiences that contribute to building a more just and equal society. Supporting their development and ensuring equal access to resources and opportunities is not only a matter of social justice but also an investment in a future where every individual has the chance for a fulfilling and satisfying life.

1.3 Promoting Gender Equality in Politics

Supporting women in politics is crucial for ensuring the full and equal representation of women's interests in decision-making processes. Women have the right to voice their opinions, engage in politics, and participate in making key decisions that affect society. To promote gender equality in politics, there are several actions that can be taken.

Firstly, it is important to encourage women to run for office. Women are often underrepresented on candidate lists, so active encouragement and support for women to participate in the political process are necessary. Information campaigns, training programs, and mentorship can help build confidence and develop the necessary skills for running in elections.

Secondly, the introduction of quota systems can be an effective tool in promoting gender equality in politics. Quota systems involve setting a minimum representation of women in decision-making bodies such as parliaments or local councils. This commitment can increase the number of women in politics, leading to a more balanced representation and the inclusion of diverse perspectives.

Thirdly, promoting mentorship programs is important for supporting women in politics. Mentorship provides an opportunity to gain valuable skills, knowledge, and support from experienced female politicians. Mentors can serve as role models and inspirations, helping young women develop their political careers and overcome any potential obstacles.

Furthermore, creating an atmosphere of equality in politics by eliminating all forms of discrimination and violence against women is crucial. Establishing safe and inclusive spaces where women can freely express their opinions and participate in political debates is essential for ensuring full representation.

Promoting gender equality in politics is of great significance for building a society based on principles of justice and equality. Ensuring that women's voices and perspectives are included in decision-making processes leads to better solutions and more representative policies. By supporting women in politics, we contribute to building a more just and equal society for all its members.

1.4 Fighting Patriarchal Norms and Stereotypes

Patriarchal norms and harmful stereotypes are deeply ingrained in our society and pose significant barriers to achieving full gender equality. These socially imposed expectations and limitations often lead to discrimination and inequality, negatively impacting the development and self-realization of women. Therefore, it is important to take action to break these patriarchal patterns and stereotypes.

One key area where action needs to be taken is education. Schools and educational institutions play a crucial role in promoting gender equality and challenging stereotypes. It is important for curriculum to include topics related to gender equality, showcase the diversity of gender roles, and counter biases. Teachers should be aware of their role as role models and promote a positive image of women and men, encouraging the development of individual interests and talents regardless of gender.

Society as a whole must also engage in the fight against patriarchal norms and stereotypes. Promoting gender equality as a social value, where every person has equal rights and opportunities, is necessary. This requires a change in mindset and behavior to avoid accepting prejudices and stereotypes as something natural. Constructive dialogues, informational campaigns, and community education programs can help build awareness and change beliefs.

Media also play a significant role in shaping our perceptions of gender. Therefore, it is important for the media to reflect diversity and the full range of women's experiences. Promoting positive and inspiring female characters and presenting diverse roles and achievements of women contribute to breaking stereotypes and building a more equitable society.

Fighting patriarchal norms and stereotypes requires the involvement of both women and men. Partnership and alliances between genders are crucial in striving for full equality. Mutual support, fostering empathy, and understanding between genders contribute to building a more just and equal society.

Breaking patriarchal norms and stereotypes is not only a step towards gender equality but also a benefit for all members of society. It allows for the full utilization of the potential and talents of every individual, creating a more just, tolerant, and harmonious society for all.

1.5 Creating Spaces for Women's Voices

In order for women to reclaim their voices and be heard, it is important to create safe and inclusive spaces where their opinions are respected and taken into account. This applies to both public and private spheres. There are several actions that can be taken to provide women with spaces for expression and active participation in social discussions.

Organizing debates, panel discussions, conferences, and other public events that focus on gender equality topics is an important step towards creating spaces for women's voices. These events should ensure equal representation of women as panelists, speakers, and experts, giving them an opportunity to share their experiences, knowledge, and perspectives. It is also important to provide a safe environment where women can freely express their opinions without fear of ridicule or attacks.

Creating online platforms that promote and enable women to express their views also plays a significant role in creating spaces for women's voices. Such platforms should be moderated in a way that ensures safety and eliminates any forms of hate speech or violence against women. Supporting women in creating content, blogs, podcasts, or social media channels gives them the opportunity to reach a wider audience and express their views in various fields.

Furthermore, it is important to create spaces for women's voices in the private sphere as well. This means fostering an atmosphere of mutual respect where women have the opportunity to express their opinions, participate in decision-making, and engage in active dialogue. This applies to family life, as well as workplaces and local communities. Promoting equal opportunities and equal treatment is essential for building spaces where women's voices are valued and considered.

Creating spaces for women's voices is crucial for building social equality and justice. It gives women the opportunity to raise their voices, participate in important discussions, and influence decisions regarding their own life paths. Providing these spaces is not just a matter of justice but also a strategy for building a better, more sustainable, and harmonious society where everyone has equal opportunities to express their needs and aspirations.

1.6 Solidarity and Collaboration

Strengthening inter-women solidarity and promoting collaboration are incredibly important in the fight for gender equality. Women should work together, support each other, and form alliances to challenge unequal social structures and patriarchal systems.

Building inter-women solidarity involves recognizing shared experiences and challenges that women face on a daily basis. When women unite and actively listen to one another, they can more effectively amplify their voices and advocate for their rights. This solidarity should be based on mutual respect, empathy, and a willingness to support other women.

Organizing campaigns and social actions is another way to build solidarity and drive social change. Women can collectively engage in actions for gender equality, advocate for legislative changes, protest against violence against women, raise awareness about gender inequality and other women-related issues. Such actions contribute to increasing societal awareness and influencing structural changes.

Supporting women's initiatives in developing countries is crucial in the global fight for gender equality. Women worldwide experience various forms of discrimination, economic and social inequality, and violence. By supporting their initiatives, providing financial assistance, offering training, and facilitating knowledge exchange, we can contribute to building stronger and more self-sustainable communities. Global solidarity is necessary to ensure that no woman is left behind and that everyone has equal access to opportunities for development and success.

Inter-women collaboration is key to building gender equality. By collaborating among organizations, institutions, and other entities towards a shared goal, we can exchange best practices, focus on common issues, and achieve greater impact at scale. Through collaboration, powerful social movements can be built, leading to systemic changes.

Solidarity and collaboration are inseparable elements of the fight for gender equality. By coming together, supporting one another, and taking collective action, women have the opportunity to influence social change and build a better, more equal world for all.

Chapter 2: Equality in Employment

Equality in employment is one of the key areas where the fight for gender equality holds particular significance. Despite the progress made in recent decades, women still face numerous challenges and inequalities in the workplace. This chapter will focus on the importance of equality in employment and present specific steps that can be taken to ensure equal opportunities for women in the labor market.

Equality in employment means that women have equal opportunities for employment, promotion, fair remuneration, and participation in decision-making processes in the workplace. Gender inequalities in employment have a negative impact on both women themselves and society as a whole. They limit women's potential, hinder economic development, and generate social inequalities.

Equality in employment not only benefits women but also has positive effects on society as a whole. It promotes greater diversity and innovation, fosters economic growth, and creates a more just society. Achieving equality in employment requires the commitment of all stakeholders: employers, decision-makers, employees, and the community as a whole.

2.1 Fighting Gender Pay Gap

Gender pay gap is a significant social issue that not only undermines gender equality but also has a negative impact on women's lives and economic situation. Many employers still engage in gender discrimination by paying women less for the same work compared to men. Addressing this problem requires systemic changes and actions at various levels.

Implementing transparent pay policies is a crucial step in combating the gender pay gap. Companies and organizations should ensure clear and transparent pay criteria that are based on skills, experience, and achievements rather than gender. Eliminating discriminatory pay practices is essential for ensuring fairness and equality in the workplace.

Monitoring wages is also a vital tool in the fight against the gender pay gap. Governments, state institutions, and non-governmental organizations should collect wage data across different sectors and industries to identify and analyze pay disparities. This will enable close monitoring of progress in reducing the gap and taking appropriate corrective actions.

Punishing employers for gender-based wage discrimination is another important aspect of fighting the gender pay gap. Implementing strict legal and financial sanctions for companies that engage in unfair pay practices will contribute to changing employers' attitudes and behaviors. Accountability for gender discrimination should be treated seriously and consistently enforced.

Education and raising social awareness are also crucial in addressing the gender pay gap. Informing the public about the existence of this problem, its consequences, and ways to address it can help build social support for gender pay equality. Information campaigns, workshops, and educational initiatives can contribute to changing attitudes and behaviors regarding wages.

Fighting the gender pay gap is a long-term and complex task, but it is necessary to ensure fairness and equality in the workplace. It requires collective efforts from governments, non-governmental organizations, employers, and society as a whole. Only through systemic changes, enforcement of regulations, and raising social awareness can we create fair and equitable wage conditions for everyone.

2.2 Equal Opportunities for Career Advancement and Leadership

Equal opportunities for career advancement and leadership are essential elements in building gender equality in the workplace. Women often face various barriers and challenges that hinder their access to managerial positions. To ensure equal opportunities for advancement, actions need to be taken on multiple fronts.

Implementing training and mentoring programs is one of the key steps in building equal opportunities for career advancement. These programs should focus on developing leadership skills, management, negotiation, and other key competencies needed for professional success. Providing women with opportunities to participate in such programs enables them to develop their potential and gain the necessary experience for advancement.

Additionally, increasing the representation of women on supervisory boards and executive management is crucial. Research shows that diverse management teams with strong female representation are more effective and achieve better business results. Therefore, efforts should be made to create equal working environments by promoting diversity and eliminating the glass ceiling barrier.

Eliminating gender pay disparities in leadership positions is also necessary to ensure equal opportunities for career advancement. Women should receive equal compensation for the work they perform in the same positions as men. Implementing transparent pay policies and eliminating gender-based wage discrimination is essential.

Promoting work-life balance is another important aspect of building equal opportunities for career advancement. Providing flexible work schedules, childcare programs, and equal sharing of household responsibilities among partners helps women achieve a balance between their careers and personal lives.

Striving for equality in career advancement and leadership requires the commitment of both employers and employees. Creating inclusive work environments where women have equal opportunities for career development and reaching managerial positions benefits individuals and organizations as a whole. Gender balance in leadership promotes innovation, efficiency, and long-term business success.

2.3 Conscious Parenting and Work-Life Balance

The imbalance between work and private life is one of the key challenges faced by women in the context of gender equality. Appropriate actions and social policies are necessary to enable women to effectively balance parenting and professional careers.

Promoting conscious parenting is a crucial element in building work-life balance. This means providing relevant information and support for future and current parents to approach their role as parents consciously and make well-informed choices regarding child-rearing. Educational programs, training, and access to specialized advice can help develop parenting skills and confidence.

Flexible working hours are essential for employees, especially parents, to adjust their schedules to the needs of their families. This allows for better time management and easier integration of work responsibilities with household tasks and childcare. Remote work is becoming increasingly popular and can be a beneficial solution for parents, giving them greater flexibility and the ability to work from home.

Companies should also consider providing on-site childcare facilities or collaborating with institutions offering such services. This facilitates childcare for parents and reduces the distance between work and childcare. Such initiatives create a family-friendly work environment, enabling effective integration of work and parenting responsibilities.

It is important for both employers and society to value the role of parents and enable their participation in family life. This requires a change in organizational culture where work and personal life are equally important and balanced. Partnership and equal sharing of household responsibilities between partners are also crucial for achieving work-life balance.

Striving for work-life balance is beneficial for both employees, who have the opportunity to fulfill their parental duties, and organizations, which gain increased loyalty, commitment, and productivity from employees. Creating equal opportunities for reconciling parenting with professional careers is essential for building gender equality in the workplace and society as a whole.

2.4 Combating Discrimination in the Recruitment Process

Discrimination in the recruitment process is a significant problem that hinders women from achieving equal opportunities in the job market. To effectively combat this inequality, it is necessary to implement equal recruitment standards and eliminate gender-related biases.

The first step in this process is taking actions to eliminate questions about marital status, family plans, or other aspects of candidates' private lives. Such questions not only violate the principles of equality but are also irrelevant to assessing professional competence and qualifications. Recruitment should be based on merit and the potential of candidates, regardless of their gender or other personal factors.

Increasing awareness of equal opportunities and prejudice elimination is also crucial. Employers should actively educate their employees about discrimination and biases, providing training on objective and fair approaches to recruitment. It is important for management and individuals responsible for the recruitment process to be aware of various forms of discrimination and know how to avoid them.

Additionally, considering the use of recruitment technologies that can help minimize the impact of biases and subjective preferences on candidate selection is worthwhile. Data analysis and automation of the recruitment process can contribute to greater objectivity and fairness in employment decisions.

Employers should also actively work towards creating diverse teams. Promoting gender equality in the workplace, including in recruitment and the promotion of women to leadership positions, contributes to building more balanced and effective organizations. Diversifying the team ensures diverse perspectives and helps foster innovative solutions.

Combating discrimination in the recruitment process requires systemic changes and commitment from employers. Creating equal opportunities for all candidates, regardless of gender, is a key element in building fairness and equality in the workplace.

2.5 Investing in Education and Training

Ensuring equal access to high-quality education and vocational training for girls and women is a key factor in their professional development and the promotion of gender equality. Investing in educational programs that promote STEM (science, technology, engineering, and mathematics) subjects, technology, and digital skills among girls is of paramount importance.

There is still a clear divide between traditionally male and female fields of education, leading to disparities in career choices and access to higher-paying professions. Therefore, it is necessary to take actions to encourage girls to pursue STEM subjects such as mathematics, physics, and computer science. Organizing workshops, mentorship programs, and inspirational events can help break stereotypes and encourage girls to explore these fields.

Furthermore, access to vocational training and development programs for women is crucial. By investing in such initiatives, women can develop their skills and acquire the necessary knowledge for the job market. Training programs should focus on soft skills such as communication, leadership, and negotiation, which are essential for career building and success.

It is also important to invest in the education and training of women in areas where they are underrepresented, such as technical sciences, engineering, and entrepreneurship. Creating special scholarship or grant programs for women can incentivize them to pursue education in these fields and achieve success.

Additionally, creating an environment that supports women's professional development through mentorship, coaching, and networking is crucial. Access to inspiring and experienced mentors can significantly impact professional growth and competence enhancement.

Investing in education and training for girls and women is not only a step towards gender equality but also a way to foster socio-economic development. It provides women with tools and skills that help them achieve professional success and contribute to the development of their communities.

2.6 Partnership between Employers and Society

Gender equality in employment requires the joint commitment of both employers and society as a whole. To achieve full gender equality, it is essential to establish collaborative relationships between these two entities.

Employers play a crucial role in building gender-equal work environments. They should actively strive to eliminate all forms of discrimination and bias. Adopting the principle of equal pay for equal work and establishing transparent employment and career advancement policies are of utmost importance. Employers should also engage in offering equality programs, such as anti-discrimination training or programs that support work-life balance. Providing access to flexible forms of employment, such as remote work or flexible working hours, can also contribute to creating more gender-equal workplaces.

Society as a whole must also play an active role in supporting gender equality in employment. We should appreciate and support companies that practice gender equality, giving them our support and preferring their products or services. Encouraging gender equality in the workplace can lead to broader-scale changes. Social awareness about gender equality should be raised through education, informational campaigns, and the promotion of positive role models.

The partnership between employers and society is crucial for building a gender-equal society. Collaborative efforts to eliminate bias and discrimination and to create equal opportunities for all employees, regardless of gender, will benefit both individuals and communities. Only through integrated actions can we create a more just, equal, and sustainable society.

Chapter 3: Combating Violence and Discrimination

Violence against women and girls, along with various forms of discrimination, has deeply rooted consequences for individuals, societies, and our entire community. In this chapter, we will explore different aspects of these issues and discuss ways in which we can take action to ensure safety and equality for all women.

Violence against women takes various forms, such as domestic violence, sexual violence, human trafficking, rape, workplace harassment, or online violence. These forms of violence not only cause physical and emotional suffering but also violate women's fundamental human rights and dignity. It is a global problem that affects women regardless of their age, ethnic background, social status, or sexual orientation.

Discrimination also poses a significant challenge to gender equality. Women often experience unequal treatment in various areas of life, including employment, education, access to healthcare services, or participation in public life. Gender stereotypes, unequal division of social roles, and cultural biases contribute to perpetuating these inequalities.

It is crucial to take effective actions to combat violence and discrimination against women. This is a task that requires the involvement of society as a whole, institutions, social organizations, and the government. In this chapter, we will consider different strategies and tools that can be used to fight violence and discrimination.

Discrimination can be addressed through promoting equality in law and policy, creating training and awareness programs, and promoting diversity and inclusion in workplaces and society. An essential aspect will also be developing the skills and knowledge of decision-makers and building awareness of equal opportunities and rights for women.

Combating violence and discrimination requires sustained and collective efforts. However, by taking effective actions and raising social awareness, we can contribute to creating a society where every woman has the right to safety, respect, and equal opportunities.

3.1 Domestic and Sexual Violence

Domestic and sexual violence are urgent and distressing issues that affect millions of women worldwide. These forms of violence seriously violate human rights and destroy the lives of victims. To effectively combat this phenomenon, action is needed on multiple fronts.

Firstly, it is necessary to implement effective policies and programs aimed at preventing domestic and sexual violence. This requires collaboration among the government, law enforcement agencies, non-governmental organizations, and local communities. These policies should include education on domestic and sexual violence, support for victims, as well as strict punishment for perpetrators. It is also crucial to ensure access to safe shelters for victims of violence, psychological and legal support, and other necessary services for their protection and recovery of independence.

Secondly, education plays a crucial role in preventing sexual and domestic violence. Awareness of consent, toxic masculinity, gender equality, and respect for others should be promoted. Education should be directed towards both young people to shape attitudes and behaviors from an early age and adults to increase awareness and understanding of these social issues.

Providing adequate support for victims is also a significant element in combating domestic and sexual violence. Access to professional psychological, medical, and legal assistance is essential for victims to recover from trauma and rebuild their lives. It is also important to develop a network of social support and non-governmental organizations that offer assistance and safe spaces for victims of violence.

Domestic and sexual violence is not only an issue for individuals but also a manifestation of gender inequality and discrimination. Therefore, addressing this issue requires broad social cooperation, cultural norm and practice changes, and the involvement of all sectors of society. Only through concerted efforts can we create a violence-free society that respects the rights and dignity of every individual.

3.2 Gender Discrimination

Gender discrimination is an incredibly pervasive issue that women encounter at various stages of their lives. It is a form of inequality that violates human rights and hinders women from fully accessing available resources and opportunities.

To effectively combat gender discrimination, it is necessary to implement and enforce anti-discrimination laws and policies. Governments should enact laws that guarantee equal opportunities for women and men in all areas of life, such as education, employment, healthcare, and social services. These laws should provide protection against discrimination in recruitment processes, career advancement, compensation, and access to resources and development opportunities.

An important aspect of combating gender discrimination is educating society about the harmfulness of gender stereotypes and promoting equality in everyday life. Schools and educational institutions should implement teaching programs that encourage gender equality, respect, and tolerance. Strengthening social awareness of gender inequality and encouraging open dialogue on the subject are crucial for changing stereotypical beliefs and attitudes.

Furthermore, it is essential to promote women's participation in public and professional life. Women should have equal access to decision-making positions, management roles, and political representation. Implementing quota systems, mentoring programs, and other forms of support can help increase women's representation and eliminate barriers that impede their success and career advancement.

Fighting gender discrimination requires collaboration among different sectors of society, including governments, non-governmental organizations, the private sector, and the community as a whole. Only through concerted efforts, monitoring progress, and changing the culture of organizations and society can we achieve full gender equality and ensure that every individual has equal opportunities for development and the fulfillment of their potential, regardless of gender.

3.3 Support for Victims of Violence and Discrimination

Women who experience violence and discrimination require support and protection to rebuild their lives and regain their dignity. Ensuring their access to appropriate services and assistance is crucial.

The first step is to provide safe shelter for victims of violence. Women's shelters should be accessible and well-equipped to provide a safe and supportive environment where victims can seek refuge from violence and receive emotional, legal, and medical support.

Psychological counseling and support are crucial for victims of violence and discrimination. Professionals should be available to help victims cope with traumatic experiences, overcome emotional difficulties, and rebuild their sense of self-worth. Psychological support should be available for victims of both physical and psychological violence.

Women who are victims of violence and discrimination also require medical support. It is important to ensure access to healthcare, including medical examinations, treatment of injuries, testing for sexually transmitted diseases, and mental health care. Medical personnel should be adequately trained in identifying and handling cases of domestic and sexual violence.

Legal assistance is another important aspect of support for victims of violence and discrimination. Victims should have access to free legal advice and representation to defend their rights and seek justice. Non-governmental organizations and legal institutions should provide such services, and the legal system should be effective in prosecuting perpetrators of violence and discrimination.

The local community, non-governmental organizations, governments, and society as a whole should support initiatives aimed at supporting victims of violence and discrimination. Social, educational, and informational campaigns are important for raising awareness about the issue of violence and discrimination and ensuring that victims find appropriate support and assistance.

The ultimate goal is to provide victims of violence and discrimination with full support to help them reclaim their lives, rebuild their strength, and find a path to autonomy and independence. This is a process that requires multidimensional engagement and cooperation across different sectors of society to ensure that no woman is left alone in the face of violence and discrimination.

3.4 Education and Awareness

Education and awareness are crucial tools in the fight against violence and discrimination towards women. Introducing educational programs focused on gender equality and respect for all is important from early childhood. Education should include learning about toxic masculinity, domestic and sexual violence, the importance of consent, and negotiation in interpersonal relationships.

Educational programs should promote values of gender equality, respect, and empathy to build a more just society. Incorporating these topics into school curricula at various levels of education will help shape the attitudes and behaviors of young people, changing social norms and addressing violence and discrimination.

Social campaigns also play a significant role in raising awareness about violence and discrimination. Through various communication channels such as social media, television, print media, and posters, reaching a wide audience and highlighting the issue, informing about available support, and encouraging active engagement in combating violence and eliminating discrimination can be achieved.

Furthermore, it is important to organize workshops, seminars, and meetings that help increase awareness about violence and discrimination and educate the community on how to recognize and respond to such situations. By raising awareness, people are more likely to report violence and discrimination and support victims.

An important aspect of education and awareness is also striving for equal inclusion of gender perspectives in all spheres of social and political life. This means promoting the representation of women in various fields such as politics, business, science, and art to ensure that their voices and experiences are acknowledged and respected.

3.5 Involving Men and Boys

Involving men and boys is crucial in the fight against violence and discrimination towards women. Men have an important role to play as allies and active participants in the pursuit of gender equality. Implementing programs and initiatives that engage men in these issues is extremely significant.

Education is a powerful tool in this context. Educational programs should include men and boys to teach them about gender equality, respect for women, and the negative consequences of violence. It is important for men to be aware of their role in promoting positive masculine norms that oppose violence and discrimination. Through education, men can understand the harmful consequences of violence and discrimination for women and society as a whole.

Furthermore, it is important to provide men with a space to express their concerns and feelings related to social pressures associated with masculinity. Promoting positive masculine norms based on equality, empathy, and respect can help break down toxic social norms and expectations.

Including men in actions for gender equality and combating violence and discrimination is also crucial for building broad social support for these issues. Men can be voices of change in their communities by promoting respect for women's rights and becoming allies in the fight against violence.

It is important that the involvement of men and boys goes beyond being mere observers but actively participating in actions and initiatives. Inter-gender partnerships and collaboration within communities are essential to achieving full gender equality.

In summary, involving men and boys as allies in the fight against violence and discrimination is crucial for building a more equal and just society. Education, promoting positive masculine norms, and engaging men in actions for gender equality are key to achieving these goals.

Chapter 4: Health and Reproductive Rights

Ensuring women's comprehensive and holistic healthcare and respecting their rights to autonomy and decision-making over their bodies is extremely important for their physical, emotional, and social well-being. In this chapter, we will examine the significance of women's health and present arguments for providing them with access to safe and legal reproductive services.

Women's health encompasses various aspects such as prenatal care, postnatal care, sexual and reproductive health, newborn care, as well as mental health and general healthcare. Access to high-quality healthcare is essential for women in different stages of their lives, from adolescence through reproductive years to menopause. Providing comprehensive healthcare for women contributes to improving their quality of life, preventing diseases, and early detection and treatment of various conditions.

However, women's health is not solely limited to physical aspects. Equally important is ensuring women's reproductive rights, which include the right to make decisions concerning their bodies, sexuality, and motherhood. This includes access to information about contraception, sex education, safe and legal abortion, post-abortion care, as well as support in cases of infertility and provision of maternal care.

Ensuring women's full autonomy in making decisions about their bodies is crucial for their dignity and equality. Women should have the right to choose the types of contraception they want to use, when and whether they want to have children, as well as access to safe and legal abortion procedures if they make such a decision.

Women's health and reproductive rights are areas where many countries face controversies and ideological disputes. However, ensuring women's full access to healthcare and reproductive rights is a key step towards gender equality and providing them with dignity, autonomy, and full participation in society.

4.1 Women's Healthcare

Providing comprehensive healthcare for women is a crucial aspect of promoting their physical and mental well-being. Access to high-quality healthcare services is a fundamental human right, and simultaneous consideration of women's specific needs is extremely important.

Health education plays an important role in disease prevention and maintaining good health. Educational programs should be available to women to inform them about healthy lifestyles, disease prevention, healthy nutrition, physical activity, and personal hygiene. Additionally, education on reproductive health is important to ensure that women have complete knowledge about their bodies, contraception, healthy pregnancies, and other aspects related to reproduction.

Access to gynecological and obstetric services is crucial for women's health. Preventive screenings, such as mammograms and Pap smears, should be accessible to women within the healthcare system. Ensuring access to contraception, including emergency methods, is important for reproductive health control and making informed decisions about fertility.

It is also important for women's healthcare to include screening and testing for sexually transmitted diseases. Regular screenings and diagnostics are key to early detection and treatment of diseases such as HPV, HIV/AIDS, and syphilis. Implementing screening programs and ensuring easy access to testing and treatment is of utmost importance for women's sexual health.

Eliminating biases and discrimination in healthcare is a critical aspect of ensuring equal access to care for women. Healthcare providers should be aware of the diverse needs of women and avoid gender biases. Availability of specialized services for women, such as abortion services, in vitro fertilization, mental health care, and support for survivors of sexual violence, should be provided without any barriers.

In conclusion, providing comprehensive healthcare for women is crucial for their physical and mental well-being. This requires access to health education, preventive screenings, gynecological services, contraception, STI testing, and other necessary services. Eliminating biases and discrimination in healthcare is also vital to ensure equal access to high-quality care for all women.

4.2 Autonomy in Reproductive Decision-Making

Autonomy in reproductive decision-making is a fundamental right of every woman. Providing women with information, support, and the ability to make informed choices regarding their bodies and sexual lives is extremely important.

Sexual education plays a crucial role in providing women with knowledge about their bodies, sexuality, healthy sexual behavior, contraception, and prevention of sexually transmitted infections. Educational programs should be accessible and cover all aspects of sexual and reproductive health, ensuring that women have a comprehensive understanding and awareness of their options.

Women should have access to various methods of contraception, including condoms, birth control pills, intrauterine devices (IUDs), contraceptive injections, and others. It is important for these methods to be easily accessible, affordable, and provided in a confidential, safe, and non-discriminatory manner.

Reproductive counseling services should be available to women who need support in making decisions about their sexual and reproductive health. These services should be provided by qualified medical personnel and counselors who will provide women with unbiased information, answer their questions, and assist them in making informed choices according to their own values and preferences.

It is also important to ensure women's access to safe and legal abortion services, in accordance with the laws and regulations of each country. Safe and accessible abortion should be available in situations where a woman has made the decision to terminate her pregnancy, according to her own beliefs and life circumstances.

Ensuring women's autonomy in reproductive decision-making also requires addressing biases, stereotypes, and discrimination that can impact access to sexual and reproductive health services. Equality in women's healthcare requires that all women have equal opportunities and access to independent and unbiased support in making decisions about their bodies and reproduction.

In conclusion, autonomy in reproductive decision-making is crucial to ensuring women have full control over their sexual and reproductive lives. Education, support, access to healthcare services, and combating biases are essential in providing women with equality and dignity in this area.

4.3 Safe and legal reproductive services

Ensuring women's access to safe and legal reproductive services is a key component of providing them with comprehensive healthcare and respecting their reproductive rights. It is crucial for women to have the opportunity to make informed decisions about their bodies and health, including decisions regarding pregnancy termination.

Safe abortion should be accessible to women when they choose to terminate their pregnancies. The lack of access to safe abortion can pose serious risks to the health and lives of women who are forced to resort to unsafe procedures conducted under inappropriate conditions. It is necessary for abortion to be performed by qualified medical personnel in safe conditions, with respect for the dignity and privacy of the patient.

Furthermore, providing appropriate post-abortion care is essential for the health and well-being of women. Women should have access to medical services, counseling, and psychological support after undergoing an abortion. This care should be holistic, addressing the physical, emotional, and social aspects of women's health during this period.

It is also important to take action to combat restrictions and bans on abortion that violate women's reproductive rights. Such bans often lead to coerced and unsafe abortion practices and limit women's autonomy in making decisions about their own bodies and health. Promoting legislation that protects women's reproductive rights and ensures their access to safe and legal reproductive services is necessary.

All women, regardless of their social, economic, or geographic status, should have equal access to safe and legal reproductive services. This is essential for ensuring their dignity, autonomy, and health, as well as for building a more just and equitable society.

4.4 Fighting reproductive violence and forced medical procedures

Reproductive violence, including forced medical procedures, is a serious violation of human rights and women's dignity. Implementing legal prohibitions against such practices is crucial for protecting women's rights and safety.

Forced sterilizations, which involve imposing medical procedures on women without their consent to permanently deprive them of their reproductive capacity, constitute a blatant violation of their autonomy and reproductive rights. It is necessary to establish strict legal regulations that prohibit such practices and provide sanctions for individuals or institutions engaging in reproductive violence.

Forced pregnancies are another form of reproductive violence, involving the imposition of continuing a pregnancy against a woman's will. Restricting the right to make decisions about one's body and motherhood constitutes a violation of women's reproductive rights. Introducing a legal ban on forced pregnancies and promoting education on reproductive rights and contraception is essential for protecting women's autonomy and choices.

Violence in childbirth encompasses physical, emotional, and verbal abuse against women during the birthing process. Women have the right to dignified, autonomy-respecting, and physically safe care during childbirth. Eliminating violence in childbirth requires educating medical staff about patients' rights and dignity, as well as implementing strict legal regulations to protect women from violence during childbirth.

Education and awareness about reproductive rights are crucial in combating reproductive violence and forced medical procedures. Increasing social awareness of these issues can contribute to changing attitudes, promoting respect for women's rights, and building a society where violence and forced medical procedures are not tolerated.

It is important for society, including the healthcare sector, to undergo education and training that incorporates women's reproductive rights and promotes safety, respect for autonomy, and the dignity of patients. Non-governmental organizations and international institutions also play a vital role in monitoring the situation, providing support to victims of reproductive violence, and advocating for systemic changes aimed at eliminating such practices and ensuring true autonomy for women in the reproductive sphere.

4.5 Equality in medical research and innovation

Equality in medical research and innovation is a crucial aspect of ensuring effective healthcare for women. Historically, many medical studies have focused primarily on men, leading to a knowledge gap regarding the impact of biological differences between sexes on health and treatment.

To guarantee equality, it is necessary to increase the representation of women in clinical research. Women should be included as full participants in studies, and the results should be analyzed for sex-based differences. This will allow for a better understanding of how medications, medical procedures, and therapies affect women's health and well-being.

Furthermore, it is essential to provide women with access to innovative diagnostic and therapeutic methods. Often, biological differences between sexes necessitate the development of specialized medical solutions that consider the specific needs and responses of the female body. Introducing these innovations is crucial for ensuring effective healthcare and equal access to health benefits for women.

Educating healthcare professionals about the importance of gender equality in medical research and innovation is also critical. Through training and awareness regarding the biological and social differences between sexes, healthcare workers will be better equipped to provide equality and effective healthcare for women.

Finally, it is important to monitor and evaluate progress in the field of gender equality in medical research and innovation. Public health organizations and scientific institutions should conduct research, analyze data, and take actions to ensure continuous development and improvement in this area.

By incorporating sex-based differences in medical research and innovation, we can achieve more equitable and effective healthcare systems that address the specific needs and safeguard the health and well-being of women.

Chapter 5: Education

Education plays a fundamental role in building a society based on gender equality. Access to high-quality education for girls and women is not only their right but also a crucial determinant of their future opportunities. Through education, women gain knowledge, skills, and tools necessary for self-realization, improving their social and economic status, and actively participating in public life.

Education not only opens doors to professional development but also enables women to develop their awareness, critical thinking, analytical abilities, and creative problem-solving approaches. Through education, women can confront gender stereotypes, break social barriers and limitations, and shape their own identity and narrative.

Empowerment, the process of strengthening and enabling women, is an integral part of the fight for gender equality. It involves providing women with tools, knowledge, skills, and self-confidence to independently make decisions, pursue their goals, and influence the surrounding reality. Empowerment focuses on the needs and aspirations of women, giving them the opportunity for active participation in decision-making processes, managing their lives, and co-creating a society based on equality and justice.

Knowledge and awareness are key drivers of social change. Through education and empowerment, we can build a society where women have full access to development opportunities, actively participate in social, political, and economic life, and have an impact on shaping their own destiny. I invite you to delve into this fascinating topic and discover the potential that lies within the education and empowerment of women.

5.1 Education as a Tool for Equality

Education plays a crucial role in promoting gender equality and building a society based on respect, tolerance, and justice. To achieve equality, it is necessary to ensure equal access to high-quality education for all girls and women.

The first step is to provide equal educational opportunities from early childhood. Girls should have access to high-standard preschools and schools that foster their intellectual, emotional, and social development. Eliminating financial, cultural, and social barriers is essential to ensure that girls have equal opportunities for learning and growth.

Another important aspect is promoting education on gender equality, respect, tolerance, and social awareness. This includes incorporating topics related to gender equality, combating gender stereotypes, toxic masculinity, and violence against women into the curriculum. It is also valuable to include the history and achievements of women to increase awareness of their contributions to societal development.

Furthermore, it is crucial to increase women's access to higher and vocational education. Barriers that hinder women from pursuing studies and developing their skills should be eliminated. Encouraging women to choose careers in science, technology, engineering, and mathematics (STEM) is also important, as these fields are often male-dominated.

Education should also be available for adult women, giving them the opportunity to continue learning and developing their skills throughout their lives. Lifelong learning programs, vocational courses, and training will help women progress professionally and enhance their qualifications.

Engaging teachers and educators in promoting gender equality is extremely important as well. Training, workshops, and raising awareness among teachers regarding equality and social justice will aid in creating educational environments that support girls and women in their development.

Through equal access to high-quality education, education on gender equality, and promoting active engagement in building a society based on equality, we can create generations of aware, empathetic, and responsible citizens who contribute to achieving full gender equality.

5.2 Skill Development and Career Advancement

Skill development and career advancement play a crucial role in enabling women to achieve professional success and economic independence. There are several ways in which we can support the development of these skills and ensure equal access to career development opportunities for women.

Firstly, it is important to provide women with access to training and courses that allow them to acquire new skills and expand their knowledge in various fields. This may include training in soft skills such as communication, time management, and leadership, as well as industry-specific and technical training that enables development in a specific professional domain.

Mentorship also plays a significant role in women's career development. Mentors can share their experiences, provide guidance and inspiration, and assist women in building their careers. Mentoring programs can be organized within workplaces, industry organizations, or social initiatives that focus on supporting women's professional development.

Promoting women's entrepreneurship and supporting them in starting and growing their own businesses is also important. This provides women with not only economic independence but also the opportunity to pursue their passions and professional goals. Creating support programs for entrepreneurial women, such as access to capital, business mentoring, and training on running a company, can significantly contribute to the development of female entrepreneurship.

It is also crucial to break the glass ceiling barriers, which are invisible barriers that hinder women's professional advancement and reaching high-level positions. Practices such as equal pay for equal work, promoting diversity in leadership, and implementing transparent promotion processes are necessary to ensure equal opportunities for women's career development.

Lastly, lifelong learning and the opportunity for continuous education are essential for women's career development. Access to higher education, lifelong learning programs, and vocational courses should be available to women at every stage of life, allowing them to develop their skills and adapt to the changing demands of the job market.

By investing in skill development and career advancement for women, we create a society where women have equal opportunities to achieve professional success and contribute to building a more just and equal society.

5.3 Building Self-Confidence and Awareness

Building self-confidence and awareness in women is a crucial element of their empowerment. There are several ways in which society and institutions can contribute to this process.

Firstly, it is important to promote a positive image of women and reject harmful gender stereotypes. This includes combating biases and discrimination that limit women's opportunities and impact their self-worth. By promoting diversity and gender equality, as well as highlighting women's successes and achievements, we can build a positive image and strengthen self-confidence.

Development programs and mentorship also play a significant role in empowering women. Through participation in development programs, women can acquire new skills, develop their talents, and increase their self-confidence. Mentorship, on the other hand, provides the opportunity to benefit from the experience and support of more experienced individuals who assist in building self-confidence, leadership skills, and decision-making.

Encouraging women to express their opinions and voice is also important. Creating spaces where women feel safe and valued is crucial for their development of self-confidence and ability to express their needs and aspirations. Through education, debates, and involving women in decision-making processes, we can strengthen their awareness and ability to influence their lives and communities.

Strengthening women's self-confidence and awareness is not only beneficial for women themselves but also for society as a whole. Women who feel self-assured and have an awareness of their value are more likely to take on challenges, engage in social activities, and contribute to positive change.

Therefore, promoting the empowerment of women through building self-confidence and awareness should be an integral part of efforts towards gender equality and the construction of a just society.

5.4 Social Support and Solidarity

Social support and solidarity are extremely important in the fight for gender equality and the construction of a just society. Creating spaces where women can support each other, exchange experiences, and build connections is crucial for their empowerment and achieving social change.

Non-governmental organizations, social groups, and women's networks play a vital role in providing support and solidarity. It is in these spaces that women can connect with individuals who share similar experiences, find emotional support, share their stories, and gain the perspective of other women. Such gatherings and the exchange of experiences can be inspiring and mobilizing, encouraging women to take action and strive for social change.

Social support and solidarity can take various forms. It can involve participation in local discussion groups, organizing workshops and training, advocating for legal and political changes, or building professional networks. It is important for women to have spaces to express their concerns, share knowledge and skills, and support each other in achieving their goals.

Social support and solidarity have immense significance not only for individuals but also for the entire community. When women act together, they strengthen their influence and ability to effect social changes. Solidarity enables them to overcome barriers and adversities, and collective action leads to greater justice and equality for all.

Therefore, creating and supporting social spaces where women can support each other and work towards change is crucial. Non-governmental organizations, social groups, women's networks, and local communities should support initiatives that enable women to express their voices, build solidarity, and take action for gender equality.

5.5 Transmitting the Values of Equality

Transmitting the values of gender equality from an early age is crucial for building a society based on justice and equality. Parents, teachers, and the community play an important role in educating children and youth about equality, respect, and social values.

Parents have a significant influence as the first teachers of their children. By creating a nurturing and egalitarian home environment, parents can transmit the values of equality and respect. It is important to provide children with equal opportunities and encourage them to express their opinions regardless of gender. Promoting equal responsibilities and roles within the household helps build awareness of equality and reinforces the belief that every individual has value and deserves equal treatment.

Teachers also play a key role in educating young people about gender equality. By incorporating gender equality into the curriculum, teachers can foster awareness and understanding of this issue. It is important for teachers to promote dialogue and discussion in the classroom, encourage students to ask questions, think critically about gender inequalities, and present diverse gender role models that go beyond stereotypes.

The community also has a significant impact on transmitting the values of equality. By organizing activities, educational campaigns, and social initiatives, the community can raise awareness about gender equality and promote acceptance of diversity. It is important for the community to be open to different perspectives and support initiatives that strive for equality and justice.

Promoting gender role models based on equality is crucial for unlocking the potential of all individuals. Children and youth should have the opportunity to develop their interests and skills regardless of gender. It is important to promote diverse career paths and provide access to various fields, including those traditionally considered "male" or "female." Gender role models based on equality inspire young people to boldly pursue their dreams and goals.

In conclusion, transmitting the values of gender equality from an early age is incredibly important. Parents, teachers, and the community have a crucial role in educating children and youth about equality, respect, and social values. Promoting gender role models based on equality and ensuring equal opportunities for all individuals contribute to building a fairer and more equal society.

Chapter 6: Partnership and Social Change

The fight for gender equality is not solely the task of women; it is the collective responsibility of society as a whole. To achieve true equality, it is necessary to engage all members of society, regardless of gender, age, or social position. Partnership becomes a crucial element that integrates the efforts of various groups and individuals to bring about positive change.

An important aspect of partnership is engaging men. In patriarchal societies, men often play a decisive role in decision-making processes and resource control. Therefore, it is essential for men to get involved in the fight for gender equality as allies and active participants. By understanding and acknowledging the inequalities faced by women, men can collaborate in building equality by reflecting and promoting positive gender norms and by combating violence and discrimination.

Partnership between institutions also plays a key role in social change. Governments, non-governmental organizations, educational institutions, and the private sector have the ability to create policies, programs, and environments that promote gender equality. Collaboration among these institutions allows for the exchange of knowledge, resources, and experiences, leading to more effective actions and impact on social change.

The media also play a significant role in shaping public opinion and setting social standards. Proper gender representation, promotion of positive role models, and combating harmful stereotypes in the media have a tremendous influence on society's perception and attitudes. Partnership with the media is essential for creating more equitable and just narratives that contribute to social change.

Lastly, social change requires the involvement of the entire society. Collective actions such as protests, social campaigns, and community initiatives mobilize people and raise awareness about gender inequalities. Through the active participation of every member of society, we can achieve lasting and positive change.

6.1 Engaging Men as Allies

Engaging men as allies in the fight for gender equality is crucial for achieving true parity. Men have a significant role to play in transforming gender inequalities and eliminating biases.

It is important to encourage men to reflect on their attitudes and beliefs about gender. This means being aware of and understanding how gender stereotypes impact our society and individuals. Men should question the roles and expectations imposed on women and consider the consequences of such a system. This reflection can lead to a change in attitudes and behaviors towards equality.

Men can support gender equality by addressing violence against women. It is important for men to recognize the issue of domestic violence, sexual harassment, and other forms of violence that affect women. They should raise awareness within their communities and take a clear stance against violence while supporting victims.

In the workplace, men can promote equality by ensuring that women have equal opportunities for career advancement, participation in decision-making, and equal pay for equal work. Men should be actively involved in eliminating gender inequalities, both through individual actions and by supporting equality initiatives and policies.

Engaging men as active participants in the feminist movement is also important. Men can support women's rights and equality by getting involved in feminist organizations, participating in demonstrations, and supporting social campaigns. Breaking stereotypes and promoting gender roles based on equality is a shared task that requires the involvement of all members of society.

Lastly, education is key in engaging men as allies. It is valuable to create educational programs that teach young boys about gender equality, respect, and positive relationships. Early awareness and knowledge contribute to building a more equitable society.

In conclusion, engaging men as allies in the fight for gender equality is of utmost importance. Through reflection, actions in the workplace and communities, and support for the feminist movement, men can contribute to creating a more equal society where everyone has equal opportunities and rights.

6.2 The Role of Institutions in Promoting Equality

Institutions play a crucial role in promoting gender equality and creating a society based on justice and respect. Through various actions, institutions can contribute to changing systemic inequalities and ensuring equal opportunities for all.

Firstly, institutions should implement equality policies that cover aspects related to employment, career advancement, pay, and work-life balance. Through these policies, they can ensure equal access to resources and developmental opportunities.

Next, institutions can employ affirmative actions to compensate for past discrimination and provide equal opportunities for individuals marginalized based on gender. By providing preferential treatment and additional support, inequalities arising from biases can be eliminated.

Creating equality programs that provide women with equal access to resources, skills, and professional development opportunities is also important. Training programs, mentoring, and support networks contribute to leveling the playing field and achieving gender equality.

Institutions should systematically monitor progress in gender equality and report on their actions and outcomes. This allows for tracking changes, identifying areas for improvement, and ensuring accountability for the goals achieved.

Eliminating biases and discrimination is crucial in the pursuit of gender equality. Institutions should actively work to create environments free from violence, harmful stereotypes, and gender-related limitations.

Collaboration and partnerships are incredibly important in promoting gender equality. Institutions should engage in cooperation with civil society organizations, other institutions, and communities. Collaborative work, knowledge exchange, and sharing experiences contribute to more effective actions and greater impact on social change.

Promoting gender equality requires systemic actions at various social and institutional levels. Through the implementation of equality policies, affirmative actions, equality programs, progress monitoring, bias elimination, and collaboration and partnerships, institutions play a significant role in building a more equitable society.

6.3 The Role of Media in Social Change

Media plays a crucial role in shaping societal discourse on gender equality and can contribute to positive change on multiple fronts:

Media should strive to portray diverse and authentic images of women. Promoting diversity in age, ethnic background, sexual orientation, and abilities is essential to showcase that every woman deserves equal respect and representation.

Avoiding harmful gender stereotypes is crucial. Media should refrain from promoting restrictive social roles for women and instead showcase the diversity of talents, ambitions, and achievements of women.

Media has a role in educating and informing society about gender inequalities and the obstacles women face. Providing credible information and reporting can help build awareness and understanding of gender equality issues.

Actively supporting social change is another important aspect. Media should address topics related to gender inequalities, violence against women, reproductive rights, etc. By promoting public debate and raising social awareness, they can encourage action towards equality.

Empowering women's voices is significant. Media should engage and support women as experts, commentators, and leaders to ensure their voices are heard in various spheres of public life.

Strengthening their presence and participation in the media can contribute to social change and serve as inspiration for other women.

A critical approach to advertising is crucial. Media should analyze advertisements for the promotion of harmful gender patterns or the objectification of women's bodies for selling products. Critical analysis of advertisements can reveal subtle messages that perpetuate gender inequalities.

All these actions can contribute to building a more just and equal society by influencing society's perception and awareness of gender equality. Through responsible representation, avoidance of harmful stereotypes, education, support for social change, empowering women's voices, and critical analysis of advertisements, media can play a significant role in building a gender-equal society.

6.4 Social Mobilization and Activism

Social mobilization and activism play a crucial role in raising social awareness about gender equality and driving social change. Their impact cannot be overstated as they mobilize people to take action, engage in public discourse, and inspire social change. The collective efforts and determination of various social groups, non-governmental organizations, and individuals working for gender equality yield visible effects in combating inequalities.

Organizing demonstrations, marches, and other forms of protest is a powerful tool for social mobilization. It is not only a way to express discontent with gender inequalities but also an effective means to draw public attention to important issues. Through these events, social awareness can be built, and individuals with shared goals can be united.

Information campaigns are another crucial element in the fight for gender equality. Providing knowledge and educating society about gender inequality issues is a key step in the process of change. Utilizing diverse media and tools such as posters, films, the internet, or social media allows reaching a wide audience and conveying significant messages.

Organizing discussions, debates, and panel discussions is an important way to generate social change. By creating spaces for the exchange of perspectives, experiences, and opinions, such events enable a deeper understanding of problems and the creation of solutions. Experts and ordinary individuals have the opportunity to participate in discussions, leading to increased social awareness.

Online activism, utilizing social media and the internet, is becoming increasingly influential in the fight for gender equality. Creating viral content, running hashtag campaigns, signing online petitions, or organizing virtual social actions contribute to raising social awareness about gender equality. The internet is a powerful tool for mobilizing and engaging a broad range of people.

Collaboration and building coalitions among organizations and social groups are crucial for achieving greater impact and scale of actions. Working together and exchanging resources strengthen the influence of the gender equality movement. Solidarity and cooperation have mobilizing power and create greater opportunities for driving change.

Workplace activism also plays an important role in the fight for gender equality. Organizing trainings, information campaigns, implementing equality policies, and creating mentorship programs contribute to creating fairer and equal conditions for employees.

Social mobilization and activism are driving forces in the fight for gender equality. Their collective effort, community engagement, and action-taking on various fronts are indispensable for effectively influencing change and building a more just society.

6.5 Social Change for Equality

Achieving social change for gender equality requires the involvement of every member of society. There are several key aspects that play a significant role in building social changes towards equality:

Education and awareness are the foundation of social change. It is important to introduce gender equality education in schools, institutions, and communities. Through education, we can develop awareness and understanding of issues related to gender inequality and promote positive values and attitudes.

Dialogue and exchange of perspectives are crucial for building understanding and changing attitudes. Creating spaces for open discussions, debates, and meetings allows for the development of understanding and persuasion of others.

Social activism and actions are necessary to raise social awareness and influence decision-makers. Organizing protests, social campaigns, petitions, and social actions provide opportunities to voice opinions and mobilize others to achieve change.

Building coalitions with other organizations, social groups, government, and the private sector is crucial. Collaborative work and action increase impact and opportunities to achieve positive changes in society.

Promoting equality in the media is of great importance. Media have the power to shape public opinion, so it is essential to introduce more diverse and equal representations of women, promote positive gender roles, and combat harmful stereotypes.

Supporting equality policies is crucial in the process of change. Introducing government policies and programs that promote gender equality, as well as affirmative actions and legal regulations, create institutional frameworks conducive to gender equality.

All these actions complement and support each other, creating a strong social movement that effectively influences social change for gender equality. The involvement of every individual in implementing these actions is crucial to achieving full gender equality in society.

Chapter 7: Vision of the Future - Equality for All

In the final chapter of this book, we will focus on presenting a vision of the future where gender equality is widespread and indispensable for building a just society. This vision is based on the belief that gender equality is a fundamental human right and a necessary condition for the full development of individuals and society as a whole. This vision is shaped by knowledge and driving forces that contribute to social changes for gender equality.

Equality is not just a distant ideal but a tangible and achievable reality. Each of us can contribute our unique talents, skills, and perspectives to create a society where everyone has equal opportunities and possibilities.

7.1 Politics and Laws for Equality

It is important to understand that politics and laws for equality play a crucial role in the fight for gender equality. There are several significant areas that need to be addressed in these efforts.

The first important aspect is the prohibition of discrimination. Governments should introduce and enforce laws that protect against all forms of gender-based discrimination. Workplaces, education, housing, and public services should be accessible to all without unfair treatment. In case of law violations, appropriate sanctions and remedies should be applied.

Equal pay is another crucial aspect. Actions must be taken to ensure equal pay for equal work. Gender pay gaps are still a widespread problem that requires decisive interventions. Governments should implement policies and regulations that guarantee fair and equal remuneration regardless of gender.

Protection against violence is another key area. Politics and laws should focus on providing protection against violence towards women, including domestic violence, sexual violence, and other forms of violence. The legal system should be strengthened, victims of violence should receive support, and shelters and support services should be made available.

Equal access to healthcare is also significant. Governments should guarantee equal access to healthcare, including reproductive healthcare, family planning, contraception, and abortion services. Women should have the right to make decisions regarding their bodies and health, and appropriate healthcare services should be accessible to all.

Education and raising awareness are additional crucial actions. Politics should concentrate on promoting gender equality and respect for all. The introduction of educational programs in schools that eliminate gender stereotypes, promote equality, and provide knowledge about reproductive rights is essential.

Political representation is also a significant area. It is important for women to be adequately represented in political and public institutions. The introduction of systems such as quotas that ensure a better gender balance in politics and public decision-making is necessary.

It should be noted that politics and laws for equality need to be constantly developed, monitored, and adapted to the changing needs of society. The involvement of governments, non-governmental organizations, experts, and communities is extremely important for the effective implementation of equality policies and the achievement of lasting social change.

7.2 Equality in the Workplace

Companies should strive to ensure equal pay for women and men. Conducting pay analyses helps identify any wage gaps and take actions to eliminate them. Pay transparency and fair negotiations are important elements in building pay equality.

Equal opportunities for advancement are equally crucial. Companies should provide equal chances for professional development to all employees, regardless of gender. It is important to apply objective criteria for promotions and avoid any form of discrimination. Mentoring programs, training, and career development can contribute to equal opportunities for advancement.

Workplace flexibility is another key element. Companies should implement flexible solutions that allow employees to balance their professional and personal lives. This may include flexible working hours, remote work options, and leave and childcare programs. Striving for work customization helps employees align their work with their individual needs.

Implementing policies for work-life balance is another step. Companies should introduce programs and policies that support a balance between work and personal life. This may include support for childcare, eldercare programs, flexible parental leave, and other measures that facilitate an equal distribution of responsibilities among employees.

Support for parents is also a significant aspect of workplace equality. Companies should offer support for parents to enable them to balance parental responsibilities with work. This may include childcare programs, flexible working hours, or financial assistance for childcare. Support in this regard contributes to an equal sharing of responsibilities between parents.

The implementation of these policies and programs not only contributes to gender equality but also brings benefits to companies, such as increased talent retention, higher productivity, and greater employee engagement. Therefore, it is essential for any company striving for full gender equality in the workplace.

7.3 Equality in Private Life and Family

It is important to promote an equal division of household responsibilities between partners. Both women and men should actively participate in daily household tasks such as cleaning, cooking, laundry, and childcare. Shared responsibility for the home and family life contributes to equality in partner relationships.

Ensuring sufficiently long paid parental leaves for both mothers and fathers is crucial. This allows parents to share the responsibilities associated with childcare and enables women to return to work more quickly, thus contributing to their professional development.

Companies and organizations should strive to implement flexible working hours that accommodate employees' childcare needs. Such arrangements allow parents to adjust their work schedules to the requirements of their families and facilitate an equitable distribution of household responsibilities.

Access to appropriate childcare infrastructure, such as nurseries, preschools, or childcare clubs, is essential. High-quality and affordable childcare facilities enable parents to focus on their professional work while providing children with suitable conditions for growth and education.

The elimination of harmful gender stereotypes that influence the division of roles in private life and family is necessary. Promoting patterns based on equality and respect for diversity plays a significant role in building equality in the private sphere.

Equality in private life and family brings benefits to both women and men. It promotes greater equal opportunities, enhances the satisfaction and well-being of all family members, and supports balanced career development. Therefore, promoting equality in this sphere is crucial for building a just and equitable society.

7.4 Eliminating Violence and Discrimination

Domestic violence is a problem that needs to be addressed. Governments should introduce and enforce laws that ensure the protection of domestic violence victims and punish the perpetrators. It is also crucial to provide access to safe shelters for victims of violence and offer them psychological and legal support.

The fight against sexual violence, including rape, sexual harassment, and sexual exploitation, is extremely important. Strict legal regulations that penalize sexual violence offenders are essential. Education on consent, boundaries, and respect plays a significant role in preventing sexual violence.

Human trafficking, especially of women and girls, requires effective legal measures and victim protection. Non-governmental organizations, government institutions, and the international community should collaborate to prevent human trafficking, prosecute traffickers, and provide support and reintegration for victims.

Promoting education on gender equality, respect, the toxicity of stereotypes, and violence is crucial. Educational efforts should encompass schools, public institutions, media, and the community. Information campaigns, workshops, and training programs can contribute to raising awareness and changing societal attitudes.

Support for victims of violence and discrimination is crucial. Providing psychological, medical, legal, and social support services is essential to assist victims in the healing process and social reintegration.

The elimination of violence and discrimination requires the involvement of the entire society, including governments, non-governmental organizations, educational institutions, media, and social entities. Through actions at various levels and in different spheres of social life, we can strive to create a safe and just society where every person has equal rights and dignity.

7.5 Partnership and Collaboration

Mutual engagement of different sectors of society is essential. Governments, non-governmental organizations, the private sector, and civil society should collaborate to achieve common gender equality goals. Through knowledge exchange, sharing experiences and resources, as well as creating partnerships and initiatives, synergistic results can be achieved.

The private sector plays a significant role in promoting gender equality. Companies and businesses should implement equality policies, eliminate gender pay gaps, strive for diversity in leadership positions, and support social programs. The private sector can have a substantial impact on social change.

International cooperation is crucial in the fight for gender equality. Countries should share best practices, experiences, and knowledge. Engaging in international conferences, initiatives, and agreements aimed at promoting gender equality on a global scale is important.

Including men as allies is key. Partnership and collaboration should involve men's engagement in dialogue and actions for gender equality. Gender equality concerns all members of society, so it is important for men to be active participants and allies in this process.

Social mobilization should be part of partnership and collaboration strategies. Non-governmental organizations, activist groups, social movements, and individuals have the opportunity to engage in actions for gender equality, raise social awareness, and build support for change.

Working in partnership and collaboration enables mutual support, exchange of perspectives, and coordinated actions, contributing to the effective achievement of gender equality goals. Joint efforts from different sectors of society lead to positive and lasting changes on the path to gender equality.

Conclusion

We have reached the end of our journey through the topic of gender equality. Throughout this book, we have explored various aspects and fields where changes and actions are necessary to achieve full equality. From education and social awareness to politics, law, the workplace, and personal life, each area has a role to play in building equality.

Gender equality is not just a women's issue - it is a matter for the whole society. Everyone, regardless of gender, age, or social status, has an impact on change and can contribute to building a fairer and more equal future.

I am confident that through collective work, engagement, education, activism, and addressing systemic inequalities, we can achieve full gender equality. We all have a role to play - as individuals, as communities, and as institutions.

I hope this book has inspired you and encouraged you to take action for gender equality. I firmly believe that together we can build a better future where everyone, regardless of gender, has equal opportunities, dignity, and development possibilities.

I wish that this book serves as a catalyst for further conversations, actions, and changes. May it be an inspiration to all who aspire to contribute to the construction of a society based on equality, respect, and justice for all. Let us embrace the challenge and act together, as the future of gender equality depends on all of us.

www.ingramcontent.com/pod-product-compliance
Lightning Source LLC
Chambersburg PA
CBHW070546160726
48003CB00005B/1916